High Fashion Handbags

Classic Vintage Designs

Adrienne Astrologo and Nancy Schiffer

Schiffer Publishing Ltd
4880 Lower Valley Road Atglen, Pennsylvania 19310

Dedication

We affectionately dedicate this work to
Marco Astrologo
who has unfailingly supported the idea, assembly, and preparation for this book
and tolerated time alone while the authors were "thinking fashion."

Library of Congress Control Number: 2007934510

Designed by "Sue"
Type set in Univers/Humanst521 BT

ISBN: 978-0-7643-2508-3
Printed in China

Published by Schiffer Publishing Ltd.
4880 Lower Valley Road
Atglen, PA 19310
Phone: (610) 593-1777; Fax: (610) 593-2002
E-mail: Info@schifferbooks.com

For the largest selection of fine reference books on this and related subjects, please visit our web site at **www.schifferbooks.com**
We are always looking for people to write books on new and related subjects. If you have an idea for a book please contact us at the above address.

This book may be purchased from the publisher.
Include $3.95 for shipping.
Please try your bookstore first.
You may write for a free catalog.

In Europe, Schiffer books are distributed by
Bushwood Books
6 Marksbury Ave.
Kew Gardens
Surrey TW9 4JF England
Phone: 44 (0) 20 8392-8585; Fax: 44 (0) 20 8392-9876
E-mail: info@bushwoodbooks.co.uk
Website: www.bushwoodbooks.co.uk
Free postage in the U.K., Europe; air mail at cost.

Contents

Acknowledgment **4**
Introduction **5**
Exotic Materials **8**
Fur 8
Alligator and Crocodile 10
Lizard 31
Ostrich 33
Snake 35
Evening Styles **36**
Silk 36
Skin and Leather 41
Metal 44
Special Daytime Styles **47**
Backpacks 52
Briefcases 55
Buckets 60
Totes 63
Travel bags 68
Designers **79**
Albanese 79
Giorgio Armani 80
Carl Franz Bally 81
Bienen-Davis 82
Bottega Veneta 83
British Walker 85
Louis François Cartier 86
Celine 89
Gabrielle Bonheur "Coco" Chanel 90
Comtesse 99
Carmen De Vecchi 100
Roberta di Camerino 100
Domenico Dolce + Stefano Gabbana 122
Escada 123
Carlos Falchi 123
Edoardo and Adele Fendi 124
Salvatore Ferragamo 126
Gianfranco Ferre 126
Maud Frizon 127
Valentino Garavani 128
Andrew Geller 130
Genny Girombello 130
Georgio 131
Gilli 131
Goldpfiel 132
Guccio Gucci 133
Thierry Hermes 157
Barry Kieselstein-Cord 163
Richard Koret 165
Lederer de Paris 165
Judith Leiber 166
Lucille de Paris 174
Rosita and Ottavio Missoni 176
Morris Moskowitz 176
Prada 177
Emilio Pucci 178
Rodo 180
Harry Rosenfeld 181
Nettie Rosenstein 182
J. P. Tod's Company 185
Gianni Versace 185
Louis Vuitton 186
Vivienne Westwood 189
Afterword: Memo to Husbands, Lovers and Boy-friends **190**
Resources **190**
Index **191**

Acknowledgments

We fully appreciate the contribution of friends who lent us some incredible handbags to study. We particularly appreciate the help and expertise of our dear friend, Carla Carosi, in Rome, a champion of this book from the start. Our talented photographers, Jeffrey B. Snyder and Douglas Congdon-Martin, captured the beauty and individuality of each bag. We are grateful for their effort.

Introduction

In the mid-1960s, a generation of young women visited their intended purchases at the Gucci store on Madison Avenue in New York. These were times when saving for a special purse was the norm; abundance was in the future. Loafers, handbags, wallets, and beautiful floral scarves showed that a girl was in style and chic. It was considered a luxury to purchase a handbag, so we bought one, and saved our money for the next. I attribute my current passion for handbags to those happy days.

My first trip to Europe was in 1966; I was in fashion heaven. London was happening, Carnaby Street was the place, and the funky fashion was astounding. But when I arrived on the continent, Paris and Rome were a different experience. Understated elegance and intentional style were everywhere there. I bought handbags at different shops, not looking for any labels but just buying unusual or beautiful stylish bags

Back in New York where I lived, all the girls coming of age at the time were working in their first jobs after college, and career fashion was on our minds. We discovered Gucci first for our leather accessories. Gucci was expensive, but not out of reach. Even if the salaries of the time were a fraction of the current paychecks, the cost of living was also much less. I lived with three other girls in a luxury apartment building on the east side of Manhattan. We were all college graduates and were in different fields, but the salaries were quite comparable at the time. We earned about $85 per week, give or take five or ten dollars. The two-bedroom, two-bath apartment was, believe it or not, $355 per month. What a time we were living in.

While traveling in Europe in 1968, I fell in love with Italy. What a place! --- Beautiful, with warm and friendly people, great food, and breathtaking architecture. Being a beginner in discovering great fashion, I was amazed. I only needed everything. All my friends in New York were coveting Gucci beauties, and so was I. When I got to Rome I was able to buy them much less expensively than in America.

One day in Rome, while shopping around the Piazza di Spagna (Spanish Steps area), I walked into a shoe store and met the owner of the shop. This moment changed my life forever and eventually contributed to my present-day handbag business. We dated while I remained in Rome for the next few days, but I made several trips the next year before I became entrenched in the Roman experience. I decided to try living in Rome for a while, and prepared myself by saving money and studying Italian at New York University.

Coblentz elegant, structured handbag of cognac-colored leather, with brass and leather handle, snap closure. Interior compartments of brown silk, and pockets. Late 1950s-1960s. $425-550

I arrived in Rome and for the next two years watched the fashions of Italy while supplying my friends back home and their friends with Guccis of the moment. I developed a sense of fashion and style, and enjoyed the experience.

When I returned to New York, we were working, going to parties, meeting many new friends, and dating. It was the time of "singles bars." We could always be found on First Avenue, in the sixties, at the popular restaurant "Fridays" (the original) and the opulent Maxwell's Plum.

Little did I know what was brewing when I started buying handbags. I was always attracted to leather quality, texture, fabrics, and different shapes. I enjoyed learning about the styles and designs of clothing and accessories. After some years of working in different fields, I found my passion in the fashion industry where I remained for twenty-five years. I started my own textiles business and worked with designers of fashions. When I turned to handbags exclusively, I bought what I loved most. Each handbag I choose is beautiful in style, shape, texture, hardware, jewels and uniqueness.

American fashion style has grown from sources primarily in Europe, and over the years Americans traveled to purchase the very prized status symbols. European designers came to America from all over the world and opened shops. Then the status reversed itself, and whoever was first in Paris or Milan when the new lines were released returned home with the newest models. Later, these would arrive at shops all over the world.

We were going along just fine until label mania took over completely. It was always elegant to have a Kelly bag or a Chanel. The well-heeled and elegant woman always bought those bags, but as the sixties turned into the seventies and the anti-war activists and hippies became entrepreneurial, women elevated themselves in the work place and more women had the means to trade up on their wardrobes. The quintessential Kelly bag by Hermes and Birken became almost commonplace in certain circles by late in the 1990s. It also seemed that all the clothing designers came out with a line of handbags to complete their wardrobes and to compete with the handbag designers, who were designing ultra-extravagant handbags, and they were selling like crazy. This area of fashion has become extremely competitive in design, and prices keep soaring. Where will we go from here?

A handbag is only an accessory or a utility in which to put our daily needs for easy portability. Yet, it has so much more meaning as a representation of style and status. As we will see, the handbag has become a measure of how a woman has evolved over the last fifty years. Her success is measured by a quick look at a woman's accessories.

The icon American designers joined the haute couture fashion bandwagon and designed handbag lines to go with their clothing collections. In the frantic eighties, American fashion icons Ralph Lauren, Calvin Klein, Donna Karan, and others put America on the fashion map.

One of the most interesting and expensive handbag collections was that of Roberta di Camerino. She was the Grande Dame of Italian style and sophistication.

Wilcof black alligator handbag, 1960s. $600-750

She had shops in the big cities of Italy and eventually in the United States. The Roberta di Camerino customer was a woman of style with a pocketbook to indulge. American women who traveled and were well-heeled knew of her and shopped at her boutiques. To this day, she has a cult following. For my taste at the time, her clothing and handbags were a little too sophisticated and definitely too expensive. I would later learn how much I loved her bags from the 1960s and 1970s. Thirty years later, I have a fascination with everything Roberta di Camerino made. I must also admit I would never snub Chanel, Dior, Bottega-Veneta, Fendi, Louis Vuitton, or the most extravagant, Hermes, or any of the other upscale European designers. My fascination is with the designs, the workmanship, and the beauty of every detail on these vintage handbags.

Througout this book, I hope to introduce you to as many wonderful handbags as I can bring from their European birthplaces.

There is a section on the wonderful alligator and crocodile bags of the 1950s, '60, and '70s, from both Europe and America. I am sure you will love them as much as I do.

Most of the handbags in this book are for daytime use, but the section of evening bags includes some by the diva of the evening, Judith Leiber, known for her eye-appealing jewels.

Adrienne Astrologo
May, 2007

Unsigned Italian cranberry-colored alligator handbag of excellent quality, 1980s.

Vintage American black velvet handbag. $250-375

Exotic Materials

Fur

Chanel soft chinchilla fur and purple suede handbag with attached fur change purse and black fabric lined interior, with zipper pocket and Chanel black cloth dust cover, 1990s, $1100-1500

Cheetah fur handbag, 1970s. $650-900

Supreme's zebra striped pony fur handbag with tan leather lining, 1960s. $450-600

Pony fur handbag with black leather, 1960s. $400-500

Alligator and Crocodile

Black hornback alligator handbag elegantly appointed with soft leather lining, pockets, and compartments, 1960s, 13" x 10 ½". $1100-1800

Cognac colored alligator handbag in very unusual shape, 1960s. $1100-1500 and even higher

Black alligator with brooch-like embellishment, 1950s-1960s, $600-700

Black alligator handbag with centered tapering hornback skin, brass hardware, and covered handle. $950-1400

European black hornback alligator handbag with plates on the handle, 1950s-1960s, $1100-1600

Three European luncheon size brown alligator handbags for daytime wear. $400-600

European dyed crocodile handbag in two tones of cream and light taupe, 1960s, 10" x 8". $1050-1200

Spectacular European dyed cream and taupe hornback alligator handbag with a moss green cast to it, medium to large daytime style, a show-stopper. $1400-2200

Beautiful skin, elegant and refined European dyed alligator handbag. $1100-1500

Iguana skin handbag, 1970s. $600-750

American black alligator handbag for daytime use, 1960s. $450-750

Italian brown alligator handbag, 1970s, $400-500

Two brown alligator clutch handbags with brass ornaments, 1940s-1950s, $400-600

Left:
Brown alligator handbag, extra large size, American made. $700-950

Brown elegant alligator handbag for daytime wear, 1970s. $900-1200

European green alligator clutch handbag with brass and alligator covered handle, c. 1970s. $900-1150

Black alligator doctor bag, style small to medium daytime size with a great lock in the style of Roberta di Camerino. 1950s-60s. $500-750

Two green alligator handbags, Made in Germany, 1960s-'70s. $875-1300 each

Brown alligator handbag, 1950s. $500-700

Green alligator handbag with unique hardware, 1960s. $500-600

Two-sided brown alligator handbag, 1960s. $500-700

Albino alligator handbag of extra large size, 1960s. $700-850

Black alligator handbag, hornback center with a covered clasp, c. 1960s-70s. $900-1200

Black alligator handbag beautifully designed, from the belly of the alligator, beautifully centered and designed. $1100-1400

Light brown wild alligator handbag, late 1950s-1960s. $600-750

Brown alligator handbag, c. 1960.

Beige alligator handbag with brass hardware, early 1970s. $600-750

Black alligator handbag, extra large, fine skins and elegance, c. 1970s. $900-1200

Two European alligator handbags, luncheon to casual evening wear, 1960s. $500-750

Brown crocdile handbag with unusually beautiful hardware, elegant and small. $600-850

Black European alligator handbag, hornback, with a flap closure.
$900-1150

Gucci black alligator shoulder bag with alligator strap, 1970s, 10 ½" x 8 ½". $895-1100

One of the finest faux alligator handbags I have ever seen. Made in the finest quality leather and beautiful hardware in the Kelly style, 1980s. $600-850

Judith Leiber karung lizard skin clutch handbag with a gold chain shoulder strap, 1980s. $900-1300

French black alligator handbag, 1960s.
$700-1000

Brown alligator shoulder handbag, rare, 1970s. $350-450

Burgundy alligator large handbag with rigid brass handle and removable shoulder strap, 1970s. $950-1200

Italian brown crocodile handbag. $450-550

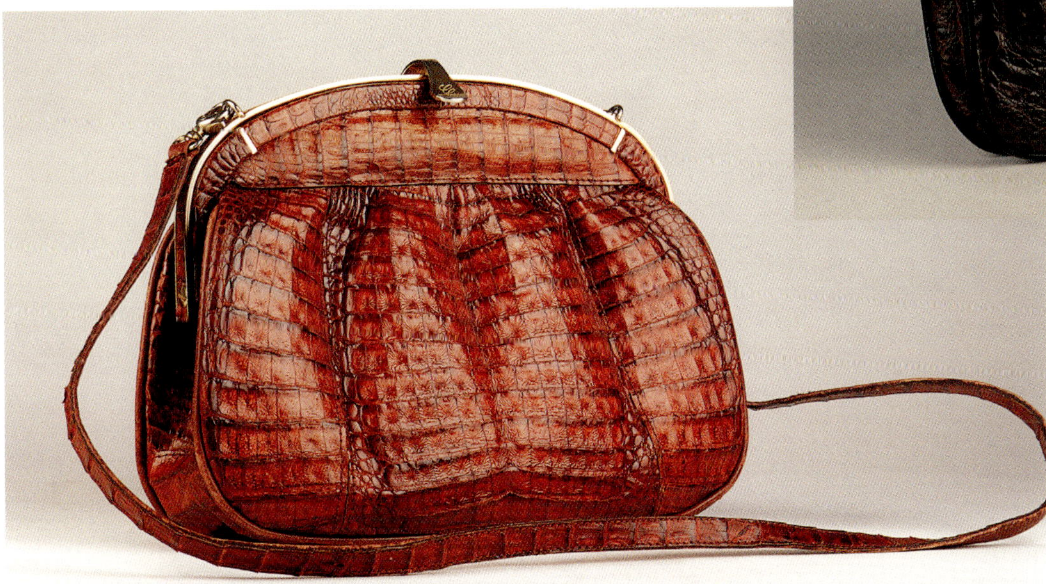

Red alligator shoulder handbag/ clutch, beautiful evening style, c. 1960s-70s. $700-850

English brown crocodile handbag with a rhinestone on the brass closure, 1980s. $400-550

Green alligator handbag, European-made, with removable shoulder strap, c. 1970s. $900-1150

Blue alligator handbag from Italy, 1970s. $500-750

Black **Gucci** alligator handbag with gold chain and gold closure with lapis stone, 1970s. $1100-1500

Italian black alligator handbag, 1970s. $650-800

Brown Italian crocodile handbag
with gold chain, 1960s. $400-550

Lizard

Two beautiful black lizard handbags, 1960s. $550-700 each

Judith Leiber black karung lizard clutch style handbag with pink quartz and crystals on the stiff silver frame, with black double cord shoulder straps, 1980s-1990, 9" x 6". $1800-2400

Bottega Veneta tan lizard skin messenger's bag with silver chain shoulder strap, 1990s, 9" x 9". $975-1200

Chanel tan lizard handbag in the classic style with flap-over pocket and embossed and stitched CC initials (Coco Chanel). The large tassel is leather and the shoulder strap is the original classic, woven leather and chain, 1990s, 9" x 7". $975-1200

Brown lizard handbag with coin purse, 1940s-1950s. $400-600

Judith Leiber yellow lizard handbag, with three medallions, rare because of the color, 1960s. There is some discoloration on the top corner of the bag. $500-650

Ostrich

Jumbo black ostrich handbag from South Africa, fabulous, almost a briefcase style, 1980s. $1100-1500

White ostrich handbag, French, bold brass closure and shoulder strap, 1960s. $600-750

French white ostrich handbag made by Sacha, well-appointed interior with soft doeskin leather, 1960s-1970s. $600-800

Brown ostrich handbag with double handle of twisted ostrich leather, European -made. $800-950

Sacha white ostrich handbag, 1960s-1970s. $650-800

Nettie Rosenstein green ostrich luncheon-style daytime handbag with flap front and change purse and mirror inside and a Bergdorf Goodman retail label,

Snake

Judith Leiber red karung lizard skin clutch bag with gold shoulder chain and 4-part hinged gold frame, closure of gold metal, lapis-lazuli and garnet-colored cabochon stone, and red skin frame. Change purse and mirror inside, 1990s. $1100-1300

Judith Leiber white karung lizard skin handbag, with semi-precious colored stones, detail on the closure and individual stones across the handle, with detachable leather shoulder strap, 1980s. $1100-1300

Judith Leiber tan snakeskin evening clutch bag with snakeskin shoulder strap, 1980s, 10" x 8". This style came in various sizes. $600-800.

Judith Leiber red snakeskin evening clutch bag with a gold frame and chain shoulder strap, 1980s, 8" x 6". $400-595

Evening Styles

Silk

Black silk fitted evening purse in pristine condition, 1950s. $500-700

Black silk evening bag with Eisenberg rhinestone dress clip, 1950s. $800-1100

Gucci silk evening handbag, with Bakelite closure embossed with a crown, was originally made for a princess, 1950s-1960s. $600-750

Valentino blue silk faille evening bag with gold shell clasp and chain, 1990s. $650-900

Detail of the closure of the handbag.

Roberta di Camerino black diamond design handbag of cut silk velvet, 1960s. $850-1100

Black velvet evening bag with enameled and jeweled gold-tone filigree frame, 1940s. $2500-4000

Judith Leiber red stitched silk evening bag with red Swarovski stones on the frame and ball closure. Gold chain for the shoulder and red silk change purse inside, 1980s. $800-975

Judith Leiber Art Deco style framed evening bag in black silk satin. Silver chain to wear on the shoulder or as a clutch. Red and black enamel and Swarovski crystals on the silver frame, 1980s, 6" x 6". $1100-1500

Judith Leiber black silk satin clutch evening bag with a closure that has a panther in Swarovski crystals, enamel, and pearl; with a black satin shoulder strap, 1980s, 8 ½" x 6 ½". $875-1100

Bottega Veneta evening bag of pink woven silk satin and unusual gold fish clasp and handle mount, 1990s, 7" x 5 ½". $900-1100

Judith Leiber black silk satin Art Deco style evening purse, clasp with a black cabochon, a stiff frame, openwork silver ornament, and silver shoulder chain, 1980s, 7 ½" x 5 ½". $800-950

Skin and Leather

Black lizard luncheon or evening, French-made handbag with a triple-loop, gold pull, c. 1970s. $800-950

Valentino Garavani evening handbag with red leather rose petal front and lizard strap, 1978, $700-850

Barry Keiselstein-Cord Persain lamb evening bag with his famous alligator emblem as a detail on the closure and with a gold shoulder chain, c. 2000, 6" x 5 ½". $875-1100

Brown alligator evening handbag of the finest skins and architectural shape, late 1970s-early 1980s. $900-1150

Judith Leiber black and bronze soft suede evening bag, the clasp with Swarovski crystals in a flower pattern with a pearl, gold chain for carrying on the shoulder, 1980s, 8 ½" x 6". $1100-1300

Farragamo suede slippers, red and black, on black silk cord shoulder strap, a novelty purse, c. 1990s-2000. $300-450

Valentino Garavani evening handbag of pink and black ostrich feathers with stone and beading trim, 1990s-2000, 7" x 7 ½". $750-950

Metal

Fendi gold evening bag in a metallic swirl design with gold metal Fendi logo hardware. $950-1150

Koret vintage metallic basket-weave evening purse with gold leather lining and a mirrored lid. Very chic, 1950s-1960s. $350-450

Judith Leiber woven gold and silver threads and gold leather clutch bag with small strap, little discs of color, and cord trim. $450-750

Judith Leiber monkey-face, flat-back Swarovski crystal minaudiere handbag, late 1970s to early 1980s. $1800-2100. *Courtesy of Dorothy Loud*

Judith Leiber silver jeweled ball evening minaudiere handbag with a red silk cord and tassel, and containing a compact, change purse, and comb, c. 1990s. $1500-2100. *Courtesy of Dorothy Loud*

Judith Leiber Meiser Pouch minaudiere evening handbag with tied cord trim, and containing a mirror, coin purse, and comb. c. 1990s. $2000-2400. *Courtesy of Dorothy Loud*

Judith Leiber evening minaudiere handbag designed as a gold gift box and silver ribbon with a gold tassel, c. 1970s. $1600-2000. *Courtesy of Dorothy Loud*

Special Daytime Styles

Brown leather box handbag with a unique two-flap closure and mirror under the lid, 1940s. $250-500

Black calfskin handbag with nine Bakelite balls
as decorative trim, 1940s. $425-600

Gucci brown calfskin handbag with unusual leather and brass hardware handle, 2000s. $500-750

Unsigned designer, navy blue calfskin handbag with an outside pocket and white kidskin interior, brass fittings and closure, 1960s. A very good example of a fine handbag that was not signed. $450-550

Unsigned designer, red leather handbag of folding design with fabulous styling. Interior snap and zipper closure, with two round leather hand grips. Mirror and change purse inside, 1940s-1950s, $450-525

Black patent leather and canvas architectural handbag, 1960s. $450-650

Black patent leather handbag with a Lucite handle, 1960s. $450-650

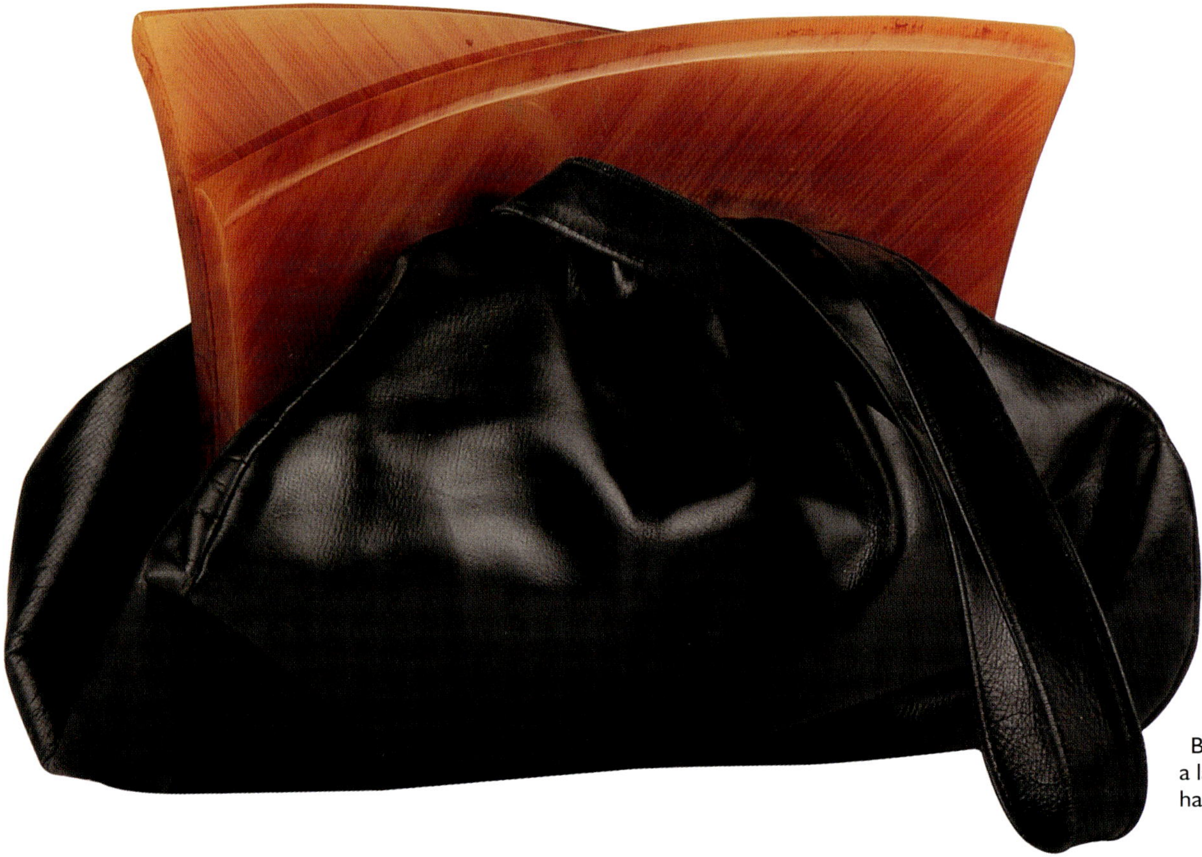

Black soft leather handbag with a large Bakelite faux tortoiseshell handle/closure, 1950s, $350-450

Dorset Rex back velvet handbag with external brass ribs and handles. A show-stopper. The handle is separated in order not to pinch when holding it, 1950s. $295-350

Black textured leather purse, labeled **Made in England**, with chrome and bakelite detail at the closure. Interior divided compartment with central framed pocket, 1930s. $395-450

Backpacks

Gucci black suede and leather backpack with bamboo handle and hardware trim, 1970s. $600-850

Gucci small black suede and leather backpack with bamboo handle and hardware, 1970s. $600-750

Gianni Versace lime green snakeskin backpack with zippered lower compartment. Handles and backstraps, elegant and gorgeous as usual from the House of Versace. 1990s, 10" x 14". $1100-1350

Chanel black quilted soft leather backpack, with a leather tassel, front pocket detail, and two woven leather and chain shoulder straps, 1980s-'90s. $875-1100

Chanel black quilted leather backpack with top flap and crossing C's logo clasp, interior drawstring and brown leather lining with zipper compartment. Snap envelope pouch in the front, leather and brass chain hanging straps on back, 1980s. $700-950

Bottega Veneta black leather backpack with soft woven and solid leather, an outer pocket, and flap, 1980s, 11" x 14 ½". $700-950

Goldpfeil black backpack, made by one of the finest German handbag companies. $450-650

Briefcases

Louis Vuitton President brief case, with signature LV logo and leather handle, elegant as always, 1990s. $1900-2500

Gucci attaché case with black leather and side panel of logo printed design, 1980s. $1100-1500

Crouch & Fitzgerald
burgundy leather brief-case, 1970s, $150-$250

Gucci soft side briefcases in two styles with logo printed design and light brown leather trim, 1980s. $500-750 each

Unsigned Italian brown leather briefcase, with shoulder strap, 1970s. $350-550

Ferragamo Equestrian brief-case, 1980s. $475-600

Buckets

Cartier blue patent leather bucket bag, 1980s. $525-750

Chanel black textured leather bucket/sling bag, 1990s, $800-1100

Chanel brown caviar leather bucket bag, 1990s, $750-950

Louis Vuitton Noe red and blue epi leather bucket bags. $700-$950 each

Gucci drawstring bucket bag, canvas with leather trim 1980s. $450-700

Missoni knitted slouchy bucket bag with tan leather trim and drawstring closure, 1980s. $400-550

Totes

Prada black patent leather tote bag with attached patent leather coin purse and two tie strings, c. 2000, 18" x 11 ½". $450-600

Gucci black leather tote bag with black resin handle, 1990s. $400-650

Roberta di Camerino gold fabric tote bag with brown leather handles and with a zippered envelope inside. $600-850

Roberta di Camerino large black fine leather envelope tote bag, 1970s, $600-750

Cartier burgundy leather tote bag, 1980s, $850-1100

Tod's red, extra large tote shopper by the Italiian design house of Tod's, with a detail of the leather insignia, c. 2000, 15" x 10". $500-750

Roberta di Camerino basket-weave tan leather tote bag with darker brown leather logo embellishment and handle. Double snap closure, dark brown leather interior with zipper pocket, 1970s. $800-950

Chanel two-tone checkered vinyl tote bag, c. 2000, 13 ½" x 11". $500-650

Chanel mauve patent leather tote bag with perforated CC design and two chain and leather handles, with detachable matching cosmetic/coin purse inside, late-1990s to 2000s, 12" x 9". $800-1100

Gucci tote bag with signature logo and leather trim, 1980s. $375-550

Gucci signature fabric tote bag, c. 2000, 18" x 12". $400-600

Louis Vuitton signature cosmetic train case with soulder strap, 1980s. $900-1500

Gucci travel case of tan leather with stiff frame and handle, long shoulder strap, brass closure, interior zipper pocket, 1970s. $800-1200

Gucci signature leather travel bag with makeup case, could be used today as a laptop case,1980s. $500-750

Fendi tan leather travel bag, 1970s. $400-600

Fendi gorgeous travel bag of black leather, 1980s. $1100-1800

Two **Bottega Veneta** leather travel bags of the same design, one tan and the other black. $700-950 each

Fendi vinyl travel bag with leather trim, 1970s. $450-700

Fendi burgundy epi leather travel bag with two brass combination locks on the fitted base compartment. Top section has a zipper top closure, two leather handles, and crossing shoulder strap. Black fabric interior has a snap pocket and a zipper pocket, 1970s. $900-1200

Gucci black leather train case with bamboo handle and detachable shoulder strap, 1980s. $350-500

Gucci spectacular jumbo portfolio black leather travel bag in Gucci's finest leather with gold hardware. $1100-2100

Gucci tan leather men's toiletry bag, 1970s. $350-500

Roberta di Camerino velvet suitcase with the printed strap, in three tones of brown. $800-1100

Buchner black leather Italian made cosmetic case, 1960s. $850-1000

Roberta di Camerino train case with red and green velvet stripe and black leather, 1960s. $850-1200

Roberta di Camerino doctor bag in soft brown leather, 1960s. $800-1500

Gucci Kelly style blue leather travel bag, 1980s. $400-650

Versace turquoise leather cosmetic case, 1900s-2000s. $300-500

Unsigned designer, Italian-made black leather faux alligator train case, 1970s. $500-800

Designers

Albanese

Albanese red leather folding day handbag with matching waist belt. This was the premier handbag maker in Italy to the cognoscenti from the 1960s to the 19980s. $800-1200

Bienen-Davis

The July, 1935, cover of Luggage & Leather Goods magazine features a photograph of Edwin Davis, of Bienen & Davis, among the "Leading style authorities" for Fall , 1935. Advertising for the company continues in trade publications through at least June, 1949.

Bienen-Davis "Brovelo" tan cut velvet handbag with brown leather trim and silk lining. Interior pockets and change purse. $275-350

Bienen-Davis elegant box-style black leather double-handled handbag with brass trim. Elegant and sophisticated. Late 1950s-1960s. $300-450

Bottega Veneta

A premier Italian leather goods house in the tradition of the master leather craftsmen of the Veneto, Bottega Veneto was founded in 1966 in Vicenza. It has become recognized worldwide for fine handcrafted handbags of interwoven leather and animal prints. The Gucci Group acquired Bottega Veneta in 2001, and subsequent collections have been widely acclaimed. It produces men's and women's shoes, handbags, luggage, small leather goods, and gift items as well as some ready-to-wear styles.

Bottega-Veneta brown textured leather shoulder bag, 1980s. $300-500

Detail, **Bottega Veneta** label.

Bottega Vaneta cream leather woven handbag with two leather shoulder straps, 1990s. $500-750

Bottega Veneta black woven leather clutch bag with silver shoulder chain, 1990s, 9 ½" x 6 ½". $800-950

Bottega Veneta limited edition, extra large travel bag, with two side pockets and kiss closure. $1500-2500

British Walker

Fabulous **British Walker** spectator handbag in brown soft calf skin. Original mirror and change purse in brown satin interior, 1960s. $350-425

Louis François Cartier

Louis François Cartier, an apprentice jeweler in Paris, purchased the jewelry shop of his mentor in 1847. The simplified lines of his designs brought him to the attention of some influential patrons and helped to establish Cartier as a leader in Parisian jewelry design. Cartier's son, Louis François Alfred continued the firm after his father's death, but Alfred's three sons took the firm worldwide. Louis-Joseph Cartier took over the Paris business, his brother Jacques-Théodule Cartier opened a London branch, and their brother Pierre-Camille Cartier opened a branch in New York. Among their famous accomplishments are the sale of the Hope diamond, the iconic Panther design, and the introduction of invisible settings for fine jewels. In the 1970s, the Cartier firm was taken over by new owners who revitalized the name and broadened its luxury accessories lines to include handbags, pens, lighters, and perfume.

Detail

Detail

Cartier navy blue leather shoulder bag with zipper pouch in back, outside pocket secured with a tassel, and interior zipper compartment with "Must de Cartier" logo. $400-550

Cartier oversized black leather handbag with unique gold hardware,interior with beautiful emerald green leather, 1980s. $1200-1800

Must de Cartier, Paris, burgundy red satchel of textured leather with hard leather base. Two strap handles and folded sides, interior zippered compartment and pocket, 1990s $900-1250.

Two **Cartier** handbags, one a shoulder bag and the other a clutch, 1980s, $400-550 each

Cartier burgundy leather envelope style handbag with shoulder strap, 1990s. $525-750

Cartier burgundy leather, signature color, envelope style handbag with brass hardware and initial clasp, 1980s. $525-750

Celine

The Celine company began in Paris, France, in 1947 as a children's shoe store. Its products were expanded in the 1950s to include other leather goods and accessories, including perfume and cologne. During the 1960s Celine started offering women's ready-to-wear clothing, and retail stores were established around the world during the 1970s. Celine later became part of the Louis Vuitton group.

Celine logo

Celine envelope style black leather shoulder bag, with alligator and a gold metal Celine horse and driver logo as the clasp, 1990s. $750-900

Celine black leather luncheon bag with two stiff gold metal handles and a removable shoulder strap, 1990s, 9" x 7 ½", $600-750

Gabrielle Bonheur "Coco" Chanel

Gabrielle Bonheur Chanel (France, 1883-1971) adopted her nickname, Coco, while working briefly as a café singer in the early years of the twentieth century. Petite and creative, she established a hat business in Paris around 1910 and befriended wealthy socialites who found her simple and flattering styles to be liberating. Chanel dared to be different. She gradually expanded her business to include clothing, perfume (the classic Chanel No. 5), and accessories, including handbags. In the mid-1920s, her casual cardigan jackets and "little black dress" designs merely revolutionized women's wardrobes. Second World War events halted the fashion industry in France, but by the mid-1950s, Coco Chanel again rose to international fame with the right designs for the new world order. She tirelessly worked right up to the time of her death.

Chanel quilted black suede handbag, 1980s. $700-950

Chanel logo

Chanel logo

Chanel quilted black leather bag with black leather handles, 1980s-1990s. $800-1000

Chanel brown suede handbag with black patent leather trim and bright salmon leather interior, 2000, and a Chanel packing box. $800-1500

Chanel tan caviar leather handbag with two outer portfolio pockets and strap handles, 1990s, 11" x 10". $800-1100

Chanel black quilted suede handbag with two suede handles, 2000s. $750-900

Chanel brown caviar quilted leather luncheon or evening bag with gold CC closure, 1990s-2000, 8" x 7 ½". $875-1000

Chanel tan handbag with three stitched double C initials on the front and a matching leather shoulder strap, 1990s. $800-1100

Chanel large caviar quilted leather shoulder bag with leather and chain straps and two outer portfolio pockets, 1990s, 13" x 10 ½". $1100-1500

Chanel quilted black leather bag, 1980s. $750-900

Chanel quilted shoulder bag with two signature chain shoulder straps and outside pockets, 1990s. $850-1100

Chanel large quilted soft black leather shoulder bag with two outside pockets and two woven leather and gold chain shoulder straps, 1980s-'90s. $875-1100

Chanel white felt sleeper bag.

Chanel classic black quilted soft leather handbag with a diagonal pocket detail and CC closure. The large leather tassel and the bold chain shoulder strap are easily recognizable as Chanel details, 9" x 7". $800-950

Chanel navy blue quilted soft leather shoulder bag with embossed and stitched CC initial tab detail over the outside pocket, leather tassel, and two woven leather and gold chain shoulder straps, 1980s, 9" x 6 ½". $800-975

Chanel black quilted leather hand bag with silver hardware and chain strap, 1990s. $800-950

Chanel large classic handbag in tan caviar leather with chevron quilting and gold chain and leather shoulder strap, 1990s, 12" x 9". $1100-1300

Chanel suede patchwork style handbag, 1990s, 10" x 7". $800-1100

Chanel burgundy quilted knit handbag with black leather trim and woven gold chain, 1970s to 1980s. $850-1100

Chanel tan leather mini-shoulder bag with gold chain strap, 1980s. $375-450

Comtesse

Comtesse burgundy ostrich bag with unique clasp, 1970s, $450-550

Carmen De Vecchi

De Vecchi black Caiman crocodile clutch bag with removable shoulder strap, c. 1980s. $350-500

Roberta di Camerino

Born in Venezia, Italy, in 1911, Roberta di Camerino is internationally known for her spectacular original handbag designs, but also has created exceptional women's and men's clothing and fine accessories. Since the 1950s, she has received the highest fashion awards and international exhibitions. Her favorite unusual fine material is hand-woven cut-velvet, in beautiful trompe l'oeil designs. But that's not all she likes, you can find handbags made from exotic satins, nappa leather, suede, crocodile, python, and even shaved mink! Her clothing designs include surreal printed jersey that resembles all the details of fine tailoring.

Logo detail

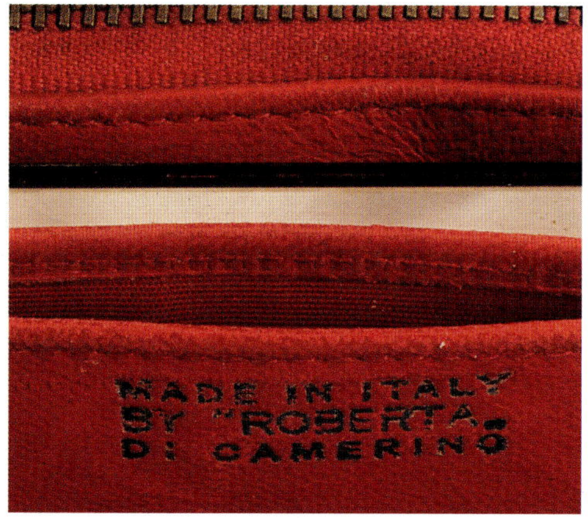

Label

Roberta di Camerino red handbag of silk and velvet with garland designs, gunmetal frame, and sliding clasp, 1960s. $800-1200

Roberta di Camerino blue cut and striped velvet doctor style handbag with two ribbed brass handles, 1960s. $850-1000

Roberta di Camerino brown velvet barrel bag, 1970s, 9 ½" x 5 ½". $600-900

Roberta di Camerino purple, green, and teal cut velvet handbag, 1960s. $750-900

Detail of the bag's closure

Roberta di Camerino muti-toned brown cut velvet handbag, 1970s, 9" x 8". $750-900

Roberta di Camerino black handbag with pink and green cut velvet stripes, 1970s. $700-850

Roberta di Camerino red cut velvet handbag with black and grey bands at the center, 1960s. $750-900

Roberta di Camerino shouilder bag of black, green, and red striped velvet

Roberta di Camerino clutch bag of black, green, and red striped velvet

Roberta di Camerino kilim carpet-design handbag with leather trim, 26" x 13". $1100-1500

Roberta di Camerino handbag with very unusual closure, two sides with compartments, and a turning closure outside the bag, 1970s. $750-850

Roberta di Camerino Italian cut velvet purse, black with wide geometric brown bands, 1980s. $650-800

Roberta di Camerino printed velvet handbag with leather handles, zipper closure. Speedy bag style, very unusual, 1970s, 11" x 9". $800-950

Roberta di Camerino brown velvet and teal fabric handbag with gold frame and hardware, 1980s. $800-1100

Roberta di Camerino black and red floral cut velvet handbag with black leather trim, rigid frame and brass closure. Stiff leather handle, burgundy red leather interior with two open pockets and zipper pocket, 1990s. $700-900

Roberta di Camerino key bag, small shoulder bag in two-toned brown velvet with unusual key closure, 1970s, 6 ½" x 5 ½". $550-700

Roberta di Camerino black embossed jacquard fabric handbag with unusual brass hardware, 1990s. $500-600

Roberta di Camerino Kelly style handbag of green and cream cut-velvet in a woven design, 1970s. $750-900

Roberta di Camerino white leather geometric-shaped handbag, 1970s, 10 ½" x 11". $795-1100

Roberta di Camerino black logo design cut velvet handbag, with stiff brass frame, front flap portfolio pocket, black leather interior and open, divided, and zipper pockets, 1970s. $800-950

Roberta di Camerino pink woven cord handbag in a small Kelly style, daytime to evening, with gold closure in the Roberta style, 1980s. $650-850

Roberta di Camerino purple cut velvet handbag with bow designs on the front and back. Elegant, as usual for a Roberta creation, 1960s, 9" x 7 ½". $750-900

Roberta di Camerino black cut-velvet Kelly-style handbag with a beautiful goldkey closure, 1960s. $750-1000

Roberta di Camerino electric blue, supple leather shoulder bag with beautiful and unusual detail on the shoulder strap, 1970s. $450-600

Roberta di Camerino diagonal striped cut velvet handbag or shoulder bag with removable straps and unusual closure, as is her famous trademark,1970s, 9" x 8". $750-950

Roberta di Camerino brown leather handbag, 1970s. $750-1000

Roberta di Camerino elegant black cut velvet luncheon or evening bag with pewter-color metal frame, 1960s, 19" x 8". $750-900

Roberta di Camerino navy blue leather handbag, 1960s. $750-1000

Roberta di Camerino navy blue cut velvet handbag with front flap covering a pocket, leather-stitched handle and unusual brass side hinged closures, 1980s, 9 ½" x 8". $800-975

Roberta di Camerino black leather handbag, 1960s. $800-975.

Detail of the unusual hardware.

Roberta di Camerino black leather faux alligator handbag in envelope style with a gold chain shoulder strap, 1970s. $600-770

Roberta di Camerino black alligator handbag with single strap handle and brass frame, clasp, and corner plates, 1970s. $650-900

Roberta di Camerino navy blue and brown striped, chevron-cut velvet handbag, with unusual hardware securing the tied-fabric handle, 1960s-'70s, 12" x 6 ½". $800-1100

Roberta di Camerino cut velvet handbag, with dual strap handles and velvet trim in a chain design, 1960s-1970s. $500-

Roberta di Camerino navy blue leather shoulder bag with outside portfolio pocke, 1960s, $525-700

Roberta di Camerino black tightly-woven leather handbag with a leather strap handle and wood-trimmed frame, late 1980s-early1990s. $500-750

Roberta di Camerino embossed alligator-style brown leather handbag with twisted gold rope trim on the frame and handle, 1960s, 10" x 5 ½". $750-900

Roberta di Camerino large black cut velvet handbag with a twisted gold belt handle, 1960s. $800-950

Roberta di Camerino oversized brown soft leather shoulder bag with removable sections on the strap, 1980s. $850-1100

Roberta di Camerino, large tan braided cord woven handbag lined in tan leather, with large zipper pocket and three small pockets, 19" long, 1970s. $850-1100

Domenico Dolce + Stefano Gabbana

Domenico Dolce (born in Sicily, 1958) and Stefano Gabbana (born Milan, 1962) burst into fashion news at the 1985 "New Talents" fashion show in Milan, Italy. The next year, as luck would have it, they presented their first independent women's ready-to-wear show. Their sexy costumes have caught the attention of entertainers, including Madonna (1993 Girlie Show) and Whitney Houston (1999 singing tour). Their business, Dolce + Gabbana, has expanded to include menswear, signature fragrances, and shops from Italy to Hong Kong. They are well known for daring animal prints and flattering clothes.

Dolce & Gabbona microfiber leopard print bag with brown patent leather handle and brass DG logo, 1990s, $650-800

Escada

Top model Margaretha was a Swedish woman with extraordinary creativity. When she met and married entrepreneur Wolfgang Ley, they combined talents and founded their fashion empire, Escada, the name of an Irish thoroughbred horse. She provided the creative inspiration and he ran the production, finances, and marketing. Their company excelled in quality materials and tailoring, beautiful colors, and abundant quantities of elegance. After Margaretha Ley died, the company evolved from a fashion label to a brand of luxury goods par excellance.

Escada red quilted suede handbag, 1990s. $300-450

Carlos Falchi

Handbag designer Carlos Falchi (born in Minas Gerias, Brazil) made his first handbag at the age of six for his cousin. After he moved to New York City, he worked nights at a Manhattan bar and wore his own clothing designs, which patrons noticed and wanted more. He kept experimenting. In a relaxed fashion period in 1974, he found immediate success with his soft Buffalo Duffel Bag design. Today, his original bags can be found in bright colors, with fur or metal trim, and resembling shapes like sculpted flowers or wings.

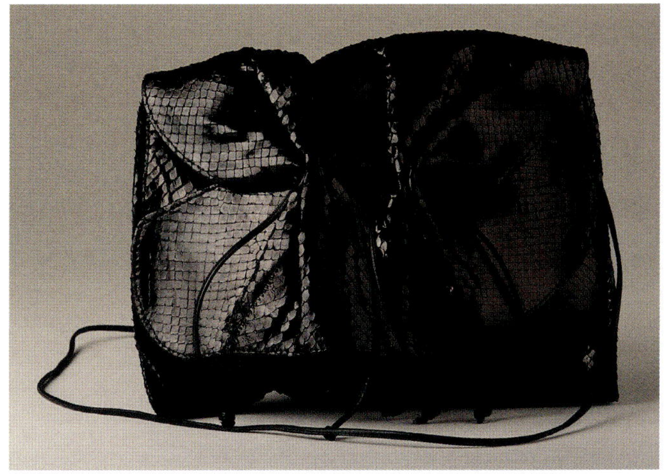

Carlos Falchi black snakeskin clutch-style shoulder bag with drawstrings, as made famous by him in the 1980s. This bag came in many sizes, 12" x 9". $350-550 depending on size

Carlos Falchi black snakeskin rectangular shoulder bag, with double cord shoulder straps, 1990s. $450-700

Edouardo and Adele Fendi

The dynamic Fendi family of Rome, Italy, has built a successful fashion business for three generations. Newly married Edoardo and Adele Fendi opened a small leather goods shop and fur workshop on via del Plebiscito, in Rome, in 1925. Their skilled workmanship and high quality materials made their handbags and fur items successful immediately.

By 1932, the Fendis expanded to a new workshop and store on via Veneto. The next generation of five sisters began to join their parents in the business in 1946. Paola, Anna, Franca, Carla, and Alda each brought different talents and interests to invigorate Fendi products.

By 1964, Fendi had continued to grow and opened, on the elegant via Borgognona, the first of many Fendi shops. The following year Fendi began working with young designer Karl Lagerfeld, who gradually changed the modern concept of fur in fashion. His designs called for light, soft, and easy-to-wear garments for women. Fendi experimented with old and new techniques for fur in various colors, tanning methods, and combinations to become a leader in the fur world today. Fendi launched its first couture collection designed by Karl Lagerfeld in 1966.

Fendi handbags were first brought to New York by the president of Bloomingdale's store, Marvin Traub, in 1968. That year, too, Fendi expanded their presence in the Japanese market, and kept growing, through the 1970s and the 1980s.

In the mid-1980s, Fendi launched its first fragrance, first one for women and a few years later one for men, and continued to grow the business, with shops strategically placed in urban capitols. By the mid-1990s, the third generation of Fendi family began contributing to the company, and today nine Fendi cousins hold positions of major importance. Step by step, this talented family continues to bring important fashion to the world stage.

Fendi brown suede handbag of folded envelope style with the logo on the clasp, 1990s. $700-900

Fendi gold woven metallic shoulder bag with coated signature drawstring and double rope shoulder strap, 1990s. $400-650

Fendi black leather Slouch bucket, 1990s. $350-550

Fendi laminated signature messenger bag that has been revived and stylish again, 1970s, 11 ¾" x 9". $350-500

Salvatore Ferragamo

As an ambitious young shoemaker from Bonito, Italy, Salvatore Ferragamo became an apprentice in Naples at the age of nine. When he was fourteen, he immigrated to America and became famous in Hollywood for sandals he designed for Cecil B. de Mille movies. They were both stylish and comfortable.

Ferragamo's wife and children kept his shoe business going when he died at a young age in 1960. Since then, they have introduced ready-to-wear clothing, handbags, and in 1998 a new fragrance to honor the founder, called "Salvatore Ferragamo." Today, Ferragamo shops are in major cities throughout the world.

Salvatore Ferragamo black leather casual bag with purple satin interior and patent leather handle, trim, and two zippers as pocket details, 2000s, 14" x 8". $700-850

Gianfranco Ferre

Gianfranco Ferre (born in Legnano, Italy, 1944) received a degree in architecture in 1969 and began his fashion career in 1970 by designing accessories. He worked as a raincoat designer in the early 1970s and started his own company (Baila) in 1974, introducing a signature women's collection in 1978. His first men's apparel collection appeared in 1982, and in 1986 his first couture collection appeared in Rome. His great talent became apparent immediately and has won him many design awards. In 1989 Ferre was named Stylistic Director of Christian Dior, which he accepted. Only by frequent private plane flights did he balance his two jobs, for Dior in Paris and his own Italian label in Milan. Ferre's own label clothing is more relaxed and practical than the Dior styles, with functional pockets but no hats. He has many private boutiques around the world.

Ferre black leather bag with alligator front and textured leather sides and back. FERRE plaque, snap closure. Signature cloth interior with two compartments and zipper pocket, 1980s. $550-700

Maud Frizon

Particularly known for her women's shoes, Maud Frizon (born Nadine Frizon in Paris, France, 1941), was a fashion model in the 1960s, at a time when models provided their own shoes for runway shows and photo shoots. Not liking the shoes available, she created her own in 1969. She made hand-cut and finished shoes that were showy and extravagant. She founded her own company, with her husband Gigi De Marco, and their first boutique was in the St. Germain des Pres district of Paris. She sold shoes under the brands Maud Frizon and Miss Maud, and by the 1980s she had a reputation for making very expensive and very sexy shoes that demonstrated risk and affluence. The public loved them. In 1999 Frizon and DeMarco sold the company and its brands to Hellene Wajnblum-Liu and her husband. The new owners added a line of knits and leather clothing and expanded the chain of Frizon boutiques to Brussels and Hong Kong.

Maude Frizon, Paris, red leather sack with front flap, draw string, brass clasp, and leather shoulder strap, 1980s. $500-800

Valentino Garavani

Born in Voghera, Italy, in 1932, Valentino Garavani, known to all simply as Valentino, had an immense talent for drawing. He studied fashion design and French at the Accademia dell Arte in Milan and the Chambre Syndicate de la Couture Parisienne, while still a teenager. As a student he won an important prize for fashion design from the International Wool Secretariat. This brought him to the attention of couturier Jean Desses, who gave him a design job in 1950. In 1955 he took up work with Guy Laroche, the former chief illustrator at Desses. By 1960, he established himself as a designer with his first collection an salon on the Via Conditti in Rome. He quickly became one of the leading couturiers in the 1960s. In 1967 he won the coveted Neiman Marcus Prize, and in 1970 launched his first ready-to-wear line and boutiques in Rome and New York. Since then, his gowns and clothes have become the choice of many of the world's most glamorous people, Hollywood stars, First Ladies, and top fashion models. He and his business partner sold their fashion business empire in 1998.

Valentino tan suede floral patterned handbag with orange leather trim and shoulder strap, 1970s. $300-400

Valentino brown textured leather handbag, 1990s. $700-900

Andrew Geller

Since the 1930s, shoes and coordinated handbags were advertised by Andrew Geller, of 525 Fifth Avenue, New York. Fine leather and reptile styles were featured.

Andrew Geller black pony fur envelope bag with matching coin purse, 1960s. $375-500

Genny Girombello

Arnoldo (-1980) and Donatella Girombello founded a small clothing factory in Ancona, Italy, in 1961, and named it for their first-born child, Genny. By 1968, Genny the company was growing quickly to become an important part of Italy's growing fashion industry that competed with French ready-to-wear makers. Genny's early use of outside designers included the young and virtually unknown Gianni Versace, who designed the early Byblos collections for younger clients in 1973; his own first collection for Genny came out in 1974. After Arnoldo died in 1980, Donatella continued to hire top designers for Genny's labels. Licensing agreements extend to many products, including leather handbags, belts, shoes, and eyewear.

Genny navy blue leather bag with zippered closure and two leather handles, 1990s. $350-550

Georgio

Georgio's of Palm Beach, mini-baguette purse. Made in Italy, brown alligator with bamboo handles and a leather shoulder strap. $400-550

Gilli

Gigi Lala produces handmade handbags and accessories in modern designs for chic city girls.

Gilli, Roma, brown leather handbag with outside suede and leather base covering, and two leather handles that join by gold hardware to form the handle, leather interior with two pockets and a zippered compartment, 1970s. $550-750

Goldpfiel

High quality leather handbags with a trademark gold arrow insignia are German-made by Goldpfeil. Much of their production is exported to the United Kingdom.

Goldpfeil honey ostrich Kelly style handbag, 1980s. $1500-2100
Miniature brown suede **Goldpfeil** Kelly style handbag, 1980s. $200-300

Guccio Gucci

Leather craftsman Guccio Gucci (1881-1953) founded the saddlery shop House of Gucci in Florence, Italy, in 1906. During the 1920s he sold leather bags to horsemen and progresses to luxury goods as his clients took up horseless carriages. By 1938 the first Gucci retail shop was open on the via Condotti in Rome. The now-famous Gucci leather handbag with bamboo handle was created in 1947. In the 1950s the former saddle girth strap red striped webbing was introduced and the metal snaffle-bit was added; both have become Gucci emblems. The House of Gucci enjoyed tremendous success that continued after Guccio's dealh. Retail stores were opened in major resort cities worldwide, famous clients gave Gucci fashion status, and the company adopted the GG initial logo in many of its designs.

Gucci label

Gucci logo print and name plate

Gucci brown textured leather handbag with a horseshoe clasp, 1960s-1970s, $600-700

Gucci black leather luncheon handbag with two straps and gold hardware, 1960s. $650-850

Gucci two-tone brown suede logo shoulder bag, with brown leather trim and gold horse-bit closure, c. 1970. $400-550

Gucci black leather handbag with a stiff frame, top brass clasp, and a gold chain shoulder strap, 1970s. $725-950

Gucci black leather, faux alligator handbag with lapis lazuli stone on the closure, gold shoulder chain and hardware, early 1970s. $700-900

Gucci black silk clutch bag of folded envelope style, 1970s, $400-600

Gucci navy blue soft leather handbag with double flap and brass and enamel hardware, adjustable shoulder strap, 1970s. $550-750

Gucci brown suede handbag with a matching shoulder strap and gold twisted metal hardware and clasp, 1970s, $300-500

Detail of the enamel hardware.

Gucci black lizard envelope bag with lapis cabochon and gold metal clasp. Interior of black leather with two open and one zipper pockets, with Gucci white cloth sleeper bag, 1970s. $900-1100

Gucci black silk faille handbag with leather trim and ornamental gold clips, 1970s. $550-750

Gucci two-in-one navy leather envelope handbag, with a removable outside that conceals a navy satin evening bag, 1970s. $600-750

Gucci black textured leather handbag with suede lining, inside and outside zipper pockets, shoulder strap, 1980s. $550-750

Gucci small beige textured leather handbag with a single handle strap, black ornament, and zippered closure, 2000. $200-325

Gucci black leather messenger-style shoulder bag, with stitching detail, a side pocket, and leather lining, 1970s. $450-700

Gucci rare black leather handbag with two leather handles, back pocket, and suede lining, 1960s. $675-850

These following signature bags are from the 1960s and 1970s and range in price from $275 to 450.

Gucci dark blue logo printed vinyl handbag with sides and leather trim and long strap, top and front zippers and cut-out gold oval insignia.

Two **Gucci** handbags. Front: small tan signature printed vinyl with brown leather trim, top and front zippers, brown soft fabric interior.
Back: Rare, large brown signature printed bag with brown leather trim, top and front zippers, tan leather lining, silver engraved shield "Gucci".

Detail of the silver shield

Gucci black logo printed vinyl handbag with top and side zippers, shoulder strap, and brass logo insignia.

Gucci small handbag with signature logo printed vinyl, navy leather trim, top and front zippers, and distinctive brass logo insignia. 1970s.

Gucci all-leather, black, rectangular handbag with side and top zipper closures, logo insignia, and red woven tape trim.

Gucci envelope clutch-strap bag of tan signature-printed vinyl with brown leather trim with top stitching, snap closure, c. 1970s. $225-350

Gucci tan envelope handbag with brown signature printed vinyl. Top zipper under the flap and front zipper, tan leather lining, c. 1970s. $375-450

Gucci navy blue handbag with signature red and blue striping, oval metal plaque with joined GG logo inscribed. Interior of dark blue leather with three compartments and zipper pocket.
$250-375

Gucci black signature fabric bag with black leather trim and green and red signature stripe, under the flap is a top zipper and front zipper, long leather shoulder strap, 1970s. $275-350

Gucci burgundy signature fabric handbag with burgundy leather trim. Flap has an outside pocket secured with a logo snap and the flap secures with a snap. Beige leather interior of one compartment with zipper pocket, 1970s. $325-450

Gucci "lunch box" details: brown leather with flap top secured by two straps with swivel closures. Bamboo handle and removable long leather strap. Brown and tan leather interior of single compartment and two open pockets.

Two rare **Gucci** Boxcar handbags of black patent leather and red leather, with bamboo handles and clasps, 1970s. $750-950

Gucci rare boxcar handbag in signature fabric with leather pigskin trim and bamboo handle and closure, late 1960s-70s. $850-1100

An elegant **Gucci** daytime handbag of fine, soft, red leather, two leather strap handles, and brass ornaments, 1970s. $750-975

Gucci stiff brown pigskin handbag with an overlapping flap secured by a bold gold metal buckle, the handle with a panel of matching pigskin and gold chain, 1960s. $850-975

Gucci handbag of Boxcar style, in blue leather with a red signature stripe shoulder strap, 1970s. $600-800

Gucci black leather handbag with blackwatch plaid wool front, a gold metal clasp and shoulder chain, 1970s. $800-950

Gucci red and black leather executive shoulder bag with an outside pouch and gold clips, inside impressed with "GG" logo, 1970s. $750-975

Gucci black leather tote bag, 1980s. $600-800

Gucci black patent leather handbag with a gold metal horse-bit closure and leather shoulder strap, 1970s. $450-650

Gucci brown quilted and smooth leather handbag with a leather shoulder strap, 1970s. $700-850

Gucci black supple leather large shoulder bag with a carved wooden handle, 2000s, $900-1200

Gucci handbag with side stitching and a handle of black leather, 2000s. $750-950

Gucci brown leather shoulder bag with large horse-bit hardware on the shoulder strap, 2000s. $850-1100

Gucci black leather handbag with brown leather trim and shoulder strap and an unusual sliding leather clasp, 1980s. $475-600

Thierry Hermes

Thierry Hermes, a French saddle and leather goods maker, founded the Hermes company in Paris, France, in 1837. The first women's fashion collection was designed in 1929 and the handbag design made famous by Grace Kelly in 1956 was first made in 1930. Fashion silk scarves appeared in the 1930s and the Haute Couture collection was stopped in 1956, thereafter concentrating on fine quality accessories.

The **Hermes** logo printed on an orange felt sleeper bag.

Hermes superlative Birken handbag in custom-ordered, two-tone blue and green, 40 cm. $9000-10,500 *Courtesy of Shahn Rosler*

The famous **Hermes** Kelly handbag with small change purse, late 1980s – '90s. $4600-5500
This design was made famous by Grace Kelly in the 1950s. It has a lock and cloche and this particular style has a shoulder strap; many earlier models do not.

Hermes Noumea style handbag of soft brown leather with a leather shoulder strap, 1990s. $1500-1800

Hermes black leather Kelly handbag in 28 cm. size, with ornamental padlock and key on a leather strip, 1970s. $2800-4600

Two **Hermes**, Paris, Kelly handbags in burgundy and brown leather, the classic shape with padlock and secured key,1970s. $2800-4600 each

Hermes, Paris, handbag of light brown textured leather with self-handle, woven shoulder strap, and brass hardware. 40 cm Kelly bag. Interior with large zippered compartment and two pockets, 1990s. $4500-6000

Two **Hermes** Birkin handags, named for singer Jane Birkin. Birkin and Kelly bags are most coveted Hermes styles. $6000 and up

Hermes burgundy soft leather handbag with a gold ring closure, interior with a snap pocket, 1960s-'70s, 10 ½" x 7". $900-1200

Hermes tan suede and brown leather handbag with a leather handle and brass clasp, 1950s to 1960s. $850-1200

Two **Hermes**, Paris, dark brown handbags, with adjustable shoulder straps, gold hardware, interior zippered compartment, and pocket, c. 1950s, $800-1200 each.

Hermes soft brown leather Trim bag in the 40 cm large size. The strap has an add-on to extend the length, 1970s. 15 ½" x 12 1/2". $2800-3500

Hermes, Paris, Sac Malette, black leather doctor style handbag with a leather handle, fixed frame, and a brass locking compartment at the base, 1970s-'80s. This handbag was previously owned by Lorna Luft, Judy Garland's daughter. $7500-9500

Barry Kieselstein-Cord

Barry Kieselstein-Cord black handbag with two handles and gold shield, 1990s. $695-875

Barry Kieselstein-Cord black handbag, with his distinctive gold alligator heads, feet, and chain, 1990s. $950-1500

Richard Koret

Richard Koret established Koret, Inc. in 1929 to design, manufacture, and distribute handbags. In 1936, Koret advertised soft, shirred designs to convey femininity and elegance with "fine polished gold finish frames…having usually only their own locks for ornamentation…A few of the bags are decorated with large script initials and monograms." Advertising through the 1950s and '60s shows the development of styles. Koret, Inc. continues to the present in New York City.

Koret mini-baguette purse of calfskin with a jumbo brass closure. 1950s-1960s. $275-350

Lederer de Paris

Otto Blau was an acclaimed Viennese designer and maker of handbags who went to Turkey on business in the 1940s but was prevented from returning home due to events in the Second World War. He emigrated to Paris, then New York, and founded anew his handbag business. His sons, Charles and Robert Blau, followed him into this business. When the Blaus introduced a line of womens' dresses in leather, they were a big success that led them to new retailers, including Lederer de Paris, a New York luxury goods company that was founded in 1898. In 1993, the Blaus bought out Lederer and took over the manufacturing business and New York retail shop. The accessories lines were expanded to include umbrellas, attach cases, and other luxury goods. As the business has grown, it has appealed to younger clients, many from families that have been Lederer de Paris patrons for many generations.

Lederer black patent leather handbag, 1970s. $350-500

Judith Leiber

Judith Leiber was born into a family of jewelers in Budapest, Hungary, in 1921. She studied chemistry at King's College in Cambridge, England,. After a trip home to visit her family, she was unable to return to England because of events connected with the Second World War. She became the first female member of the Hungarian Handbag Guild. Judith came with her family to the United States in 1946.

Judith and her husband, Gus, founded their handbag company in 1963. Designed and handmade by a small staff, distinctive beaded minaudiere bags became her most famous designs initially. Those for day use include exotic karung snake, alligator, whip snake, and calfskin in imaginative styles. Later, clever evening bags covered with crystals were made and sold out quickly. Today, Judith Leiber handbags are expensive treasures considered to be collectors' items that appear in the collections of decorative arts museums.

One of the first handbags made by **Judith Leiber**, an evening bag that also can be used as a jewelry case on the dressing table, the designer's name signed in gold on the inside, 1950-'60.

Judith Leiber label detail

Judith Leiber green leather handbag, 1980s. $350-500

Judith Leiber red jeweled briefcase-style evening handbag in Swarovski crystal. $1200-1900

Judith Leiber navy blue karong lizard handbag with stitched chevrons and gold patterned flap and detachable shoulder strap and change purse, c. 1980s. $750-950

Judith Leiber karong lizard handbag with a jeweled dragonfly detail and removable silk cord shoulder strap, with balls at the ends and comb and mirror accessories, 1980s. $1500-2500

Judith Leiber sewn black snakeskin clutch bag, with an ornamented front flap, detachable shoulder strap, side pocket, zipper compartment, and change purse. $700-900
Judith Leiber back leather handbag with a brass top clasp and a shoulder strap, c. 1970s. $450-700

Judith Leiber black alligator handbag, with four balls ornamented with black crystals, and double handle, 1980s. $1400-2100

A great **Judith Leiber** tan lizard handbag that has a valuables compartment in the base that opens independently and contains a cosmetic mirror in its own grey sleeper sack. A separate detachable shoulder strap is included. $1200-1500

Judith Leiber black lizard handbag, with individual semi-precious stone ornaments on the gold frame, 1970s. $400-650

Judith Leiber tan snakeskin clutch bag with a gold chain shoulder strap, gold frame with tiger eye stone clasp, $600-800
Judith Leiber black snakeskin clutch bag with a gold frame and black snakeskin clasp. $500-700.

Judith Leiber tan embroidered snakeskin handbag for daytime into evening use, with zipper top and gold hardware, 1980s. $600-800

Judith Leiber cream colored soft leather handbag with ribbed brass frame and cabochon moonstones, inside are a compact and change purse, 1980s. $650-900

Judith Leiber black quilted leather handbag, with an adjustable leather shoulder strap, 1980s. $500-650

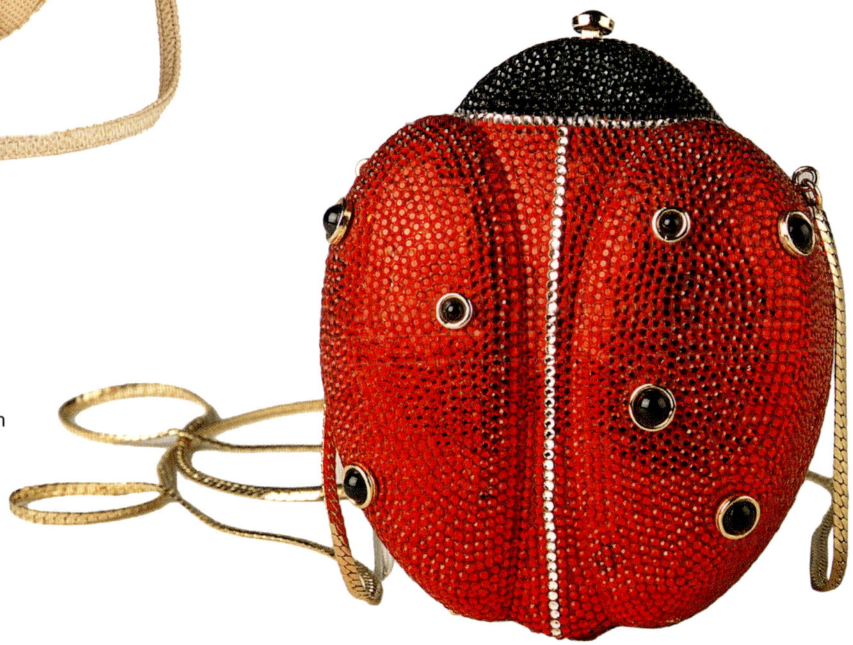

Judith Leiber ladybug minaudier with red, black, and clear Swarovski crystal flatback and semi-precious stones as ornaments, and inside a comb, change purse, and mirror, with a silver chain shoulder strap, c. 2000. $2500-3500

Lucille de Paris

Lucille de Paris interior label detail.

Lucille de Paris caramel alligator handbag with frame and single handle, 1960s. $800-1200

Lucille de Paris black calf leather handbag in the classic Kelly style, 1960s. $500-750 Truly a magnificaent work of art.

Two handbags by **Lucille de Paris**, a tan ostrich leather Kelly style with marvelous interiors or fitted compartments, zippers, snaps; self-covered frame and double handle, and a white ostrich style with a single self handle, 1960s. $700-950. One of the best American handbag designers.

Rosita and Ottavio Missoni

The fashion design firm Missoni evolved from the passions of its talented founders Rosita Jelmini (born near Varese, Italy in 1932) and Ottavio "Tai" Missoni (born in Dalmatia in 1921 and brought up in Trieste). Rosita was in London to improve her English in 1948 when she attended the Olympic games in London and watched Ottavio run the 400 meters obstacle course. She decided then that he would become her husband, and in 1953 they were married. Ottavio had produced the tracksuits worn by the Italian national team at the 1948 Olympics, and continued in that business after the games were over.

The transition from track suits to knitwear was gradual but deliberate, and in 1964 the Missonis met designer Emmanuelle Kahn. Together, they created a knitwear collection that they showed in Milan in 1966, and another collection in 1967 at the Pitti Palace. They made headlines, because at the last minute Rosita told the models to take off their bras because they ruined the lines of the black silk jersey dresses. Missoni didn't know that under the Pitti's blazing lights, the tops of the dresses would become transparent. The fashion world was shocked.

Knitwear lent itself to colorful designs, and Missoni sometimes looked to folk arts for inspiration. The company has grown in stature, variety of textiles, and size through the years and now employs Rosita and Ottavio's the three children, who have leading roles in its current success.

Missoni textured synthetic material briefcase, with leather handles, trim and interior, 1990s. $300-500

Morris Moskowitz

Morris Moskowitz Corp. was organized in 1948 to begin the "MM" label. Handbags and large totes were their specialty, in dramatic fabrics. Velveteen, flannel, corduroy, fake fur, and paisley prints, some with leather trim, were featured.

MM, Morris Moskowitz bone colored and textured leather handbag with gold trim and a double handle. Original, elegant, lady-like design, not one of the highest-end bags but always a solid designer with a price that was usually affordable, 1980s. $350-425

MM, Morris Moskowitz black textured leather handbag with a clasp of colored stones signed by costume jewelry designer Marcel Boucher, 1960s-1970s. $500-600

Prada

Mario Prada founded his business in leather handbags, shoes, trunks, and suitcases in 1913 in Milan, Italy. His granddaughter, Miuccia Prada, had been making smart nylon backpacks since 1970, and took over the Prada company in 1978. By 1985, Prada had gained an international reputation for sleek and practical handbag and garment designs in elegant materials to compete with the finest fashion houses. A more affordable Miu Miu line was brought out in 1992 for Prada's younger customers. It featured more flowing shapes and earth colors, but kept the Prada classic appearance intact. In 1993, Prada earned the Council of Fashion Designers of America award for accessories. Now Prada boutiques in dozens of cities worldwide offer their elegant fashions with the distinctive Prada silver triangle status symbol.

Prada Miu Miu line, brown leather Hobo handbag with brown suede interior, 2000. $450-600

Emilio Pucci

Marchese Emilio Pucci di Barsento was born in 1914 in Naples, Italy, the son of a wealthy aristocrat. He was raised in the lap of luxury, became an avid skier and scholar, earning a PhD in Political Science, and joined th Italian Olympic ski team in 1934. In 1935, Pucci earned a skiing scholarship and attended a university in the United States, where he first designed sportswear for his ski team. He was a pilot for the Italian Air Force during the Second World War.

While skiing on the slopes of St. Moritz, a reporter from Harper's Bazaar magazine notice Pucci in his unusual outfit and took a few photos. Her editor learned that Pucci had designed his skiwear and invited him to create some pieces for a photo session about winter fashion. The designs were featured in the Winter 1948 edition of Harper's Bazaar, where Pucci's style and taste was first presented. In 1949, he opened his first shop in Capri, and in 1950 created a couture line of clothing in bold colors and prints on lightweight fabrics. Emilio Pucci was then the first in his family to hold gainful employment in over a thousand years.

Pucci designed casual wear from Capri pants to silk scarves, dresses, handbags, and pajamas. His bold and striking prints were instantly popular with the jet-set crowd, who found the lightweight and wrinkle-free clothing perfect for travel.

In the 1950s and '60s, Pucci prints revolutionized fashion. Today, original prints are highly collected, and the current line of Pucci clothing is still in demand by customers.

Emilio Pucci printed velvet handbag by Jana, Made in Italy. Signature pattern in a purple velvet combination and front flap, with leather-covered handle, brass hardware, and red leather lining, 1960s. $750-950

Emilio Pucci printed silk blue design in a small and elegant evening purse of hard box shape with six stiff gold colored brass twisted ropes for the handle. A real gem, with beautiful green leather lining, 1960s. $650-800

Emilio Pucci handbag in multi-colored printed silk with a double gold chain handle, 1960s. $650-850

Emilio Pucci handbag in pink patterned printed silk with a self-covered fabric handle, 1960s. $650-800

Rodo

Rodo of Italy navy blue leather handbag, with side pocket and adjustable leather shoulder strap with brass hardware, 1970s. $500-650

Rodo, Italian, black basket-weave straw clutch purse with gold clasp and shoulder chain, 1960s-'70s, 11 ½" x 6 ½". $125-195

Rodo, Italian, white basket-weave straw clutch purse, 1960s-70s, 8" x 5 ½". $90-150

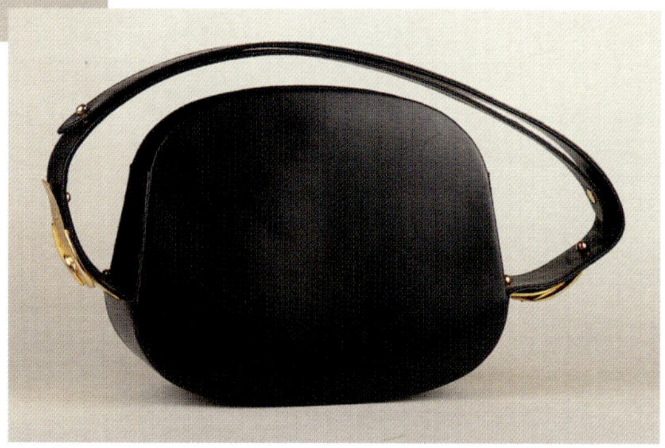

Harry Rosenfeld

Harry Rosenfeld was making notable handbags in 1955. He sought designs with striking silhouettes, such as pinwheels, binoculars, and Aladdin's lamps. Some had a large opening covered with an oval frame, others had oblong shape with two openings. He included odd handles, off-center locks, and trimmed openings for variety. Rosenfeld's materials included elegant and luster leather as well as clear vinyl and linen.

Harry Rosenfeld black rouched leather handbag with a distinctive scalloped Bakelite closure, 1940s. $500-750

Harry Rosenfeld brown suede handbag of triangular shape with an unusual mother-of-pearl catch and a self-handle with knotted accents, 1950s. $300-400

Nettie Rosenstein

Nettie Rosenstein was born in the Austro-Hungarian Empire and emigrated to New York City as a child in the 1890s. She married Saul Rosenstein in 1916 and casually started a dressmaking business in her house for friends. By 1921, Nettie moved to midtown Manhattan, where she employed a staff of fifty. After I. Magnin women's store placed an ample order for her dresses, she began wholesaling, but she permitted only one store in each city to use her label. In the early 1940s, her black crepe dresses for daytime had bare necklines that could be worn with jewelry in the evenings. Thereby, she originated "the little black dress."

Nettie Rosenstein label detail

Nettie Rosenstein black leather handbag with self-handle and elegant shape, 1950s-60s. $400-550

Nettie Rosenstein Kelly style leather handbag with shaded brown bargello needlepoint front and folding flap and a leather handle, 1960s. $400-600

Nettie Rosenstein olive green smooth leather handbag with a deep flap and self-handle and leather closure, a change purse and mirror within, 1950s-'60s. $400-550

Nettie Rosenstein olive green smooth leather handbag with a short flap and self-handle and sliding leather clasp, again a mirror and change purse within, 1950s-'60s. $400-550

J. P. Tod's Company

The J. P. Tod's Company, of Italy, is well known for luxurious leather goods, such as handbags and shoes. Their boutiques in Rome are a shopping destination for current style-conscious customers.

Tod's of Italy brown leather casual handbag with mustard colored leather trim, late 1990s. $400-600

Gianni Versace

Born in Reggio Calabria, Italy, in 1946, Gianni Versace learned much from his mother's dressmaking business and became a freelance designer. By 1971, he was creating collections for top fashion houses Genny, Complice, and Callaghan. With help from his brother, Santo, he founded the Gianni Versace company in 1978 and showed his first collection for women in Milan. Awards came quickly, from Cutty Sark (1982, 1988) and Golden Eye (L'Occio d'Oro, 1982, 1984, 990, 1991). During the 1980s he also designed costumes for theatrical productions at Theatro della Scala and other top venues. Versace opened his flagship boutique in Berlin in 1994, and began a series of books about his designs with the world's top photographers. He was at the very top of his field when he was tragically murdered in front of his home in Miami, Florida, in July of 1997. Versace's brother and sister, Santo and Donatella Versace, continued his business after his death, Donatella becoming the new head of design.

Gianni Versace lime green pigskin leather shoulder bag with two matching straps and gold metal frame, c. 2000, 14" x 12". $700-900.

Louis Vuitton

Louis Vuitton (born 1821 in Anchay, Jura, France, died 1892) was apprenticed to several luggage makers in Paris from 1837 before he founded his own company and began making trunks in 1854. His flat luggage designs were distinctive for their intended use on the new railway cars for personal travel; traditional iron-bound trunks were used on horse-drawn coaches. He expanded his factory and relocated to Asniéres in 1860. Vuitton luggage gained international recognition, in part to the awarding of a bronze medal at the 1867 World's Fair and a gold medal at the 1889 World's Fair, both in Paris. '

After Louis died in 1892, his son, Georges, took over the company and put a stop to widespread copying of Vuitton designs by developing and patenting the distinctive "LV" monogram in beige on chestnut brown leather, thereby creating the first designer label on a product. Georges also developed Vuitton's unique five-combination lock. The company grew in size and importance by keeping the quality of their luxury goods of the highest standards.

When Georges died in 1936, his son, Gaston-Louis, headed the company through the difficult years of the Second World War. The Louis Vuitton company has become a leader in luxury consumer goods, with products that include handbags, travel books, perfume, and designer clothing.

Two styles of **Louis Vuitton** Alma and Speedy bags, each with logo-printed brown signature print and light plain leather trim, handles, and zipper closures, 1980s. $400-600

Louis Vuitton black epi leather handbag with two hinged handles and brass zipper closure, 1990s. $450-600

Louis Vuitton Nil classic brown logo print camera bag, zippered top, shoulder bag with brown leather trim and adjustable shoulder strap, 1980s.

Two small **Louis Vuitton** pochette clutch bags with the standard LV print, the white one was created for Louis Vuitton by Takashi Murakami. $250-400

Louis Vuitton black epi leather pochette clutch with zippered top closure and an optional, adjustable leather shoulder strap, 2000s. $300-400

Louis Vuitton Saumur shoulder bag, resembling a saddle bag, of logo-print and solid leather trim, with unusual adjustable side straps, medium size of the four sizes in this most popular bag, 1980s. $550-1500 depending on size

Vivienne Westwood

Born in Glossop, Derbyshire, England, in 1941, Vivienne Westwood began designing clothes in 1971 and opened her first shop, Let It Rock, in London. The shop underwent changes of name and style, emerging in 1974 with the name Sex, a boutique selling bondage gear and other attire connected with the punk style. Westwood showed her first clothing collection in 1981 in London, and in 1983 she had a show in Paris. In 1984 she burst on the Japanese market, where her clothes are still best loved. She launched a menswear collection in Florence in 1990 and was named British Designer of the Year. Her provocative and daring styles continue to make headlines.

Vivienne Westwood tote bag of red and blue plaid material and two self-handles, 1990s. $350-550

Afterword

Memo to Husbands, Lovers, and Boyfriends

We women love our toys, just like you do yours. When we see a beautiful handbag that speaks to us and you tell us we don't need it, or "let's go," you are denying some of the small pleasures that we so enjoy. Women really don't like having to smuggle in our treasures or tell you this was in the closet.

Men, listen up! We love our girl toys, so make it a point to acknowledge us and appreciate our passions. We consciously recognize your passions, so please accept ours. Start with a beautiful handbag.

We would like to give thanks to the few "good" guys who willingly champion our interests in fashion. We hope somewhere in time that more of you will understand our quirks.

Resources

Books

Chenoune, Farid. *Carried Away, all about bags*. Paris-New York: Le Passage, 2004.

Higgins, Paula and Lori Blaser. *A Passion for Purses: 1600-2005*. Atglen, Pennsylvania: Schiffer Publishing, 2006.

Smith, Desire. *Handbag Chic*. Atglen, Pennsylvania: Schiffer Publishing, 2005.

Internet

answers.com
bagladyemporium.com
cjh.com
designer-fashion-trends.com
diplomatie.gouv.fr
fashionmission.nl
fashionmodeldirectory.com
fragrancewholesale.com
fragrancex.com
fundinguniverse.com
henriettashandbags.com
home.eol.ca
lifeinitaly.com
myspace.com
nysun.com
searchwarp.com
wikipedia.org
womenshistory.about.com

Index

Albanese 79
alligator skin 10-29, 43, 126, 169
Armani, Giorgio 80
attaché case 56
backpacks 52-54
Bally, Carl Franz 81
Bergdorf Goodman 34
Bienen-Davis 82
Blau, Otto 165
Bottega Veneta 31, 40, 54, 72, 83, 84
Boucher, Marcel 177
briefcases 55-59, 176
British Walker 85
Buchner 76
bucket bags 60-62
Cartier, Louis François 60, 63, 86-88
Celine, 89
Cerruti, Nino 80
Chanel, Gabrielle Bonheur "Coco" 8, 32, 53, 60, 66, 80, 90-98
cheetah fur 9
chinchilla fur 8
Comtesse 99
crocodile skin 10-29, 30, 78
Crouch & Fitzgerald 57
De Vecci, Carmen 100
DeMarco, Gigi 127
di Camerino, Roberta 38, 63, 64, 65, 75, 76, 100-121
Dior, Christian 80
Dolce + Gabbana 122
Dolce, Domenico 122
Dorset Rex 51
Eisenberg clip 37
Escada 123
Falchi, Carlos 123
Fendi 44, 71, 72, 73, 124, 125
Fendi, Adele 124
Fendi, Edouardo 124
Ferragamo, Salvatore 43, 59, 126
Ferre, Gianfranco 126
Frizon, Maud 127
fur 8, 9, 42
Gabbana, Stefano 122
Galeotti, Sergio 80
Garavani, Valentino 37, 41, 43, 128
Geller, Andrew 130
Genny 130
Georgio's of Palm Beach 131
Gilli 131
Girombello, Arnoldo 130
Girombello, Donatella 130
Goldpfeil 54, 132
Gucci, Guccio 25, 29, 37, 49, 52, 56, 58, 62, 63, 67, 69, 70, 74, 77, 133-156
Hermes 157-162
Hermes, Thierry 157
iguana skin 15
karung lizard skin 31, 35, 167, 168
Keiselstein-Cord, Barry 42, 163, 164
Kelly style 25, 110, 132, 158, 159, 174, 175, 182
Koret, Richard 45, 165
Lala, Gilli 131
lamb fur 42
Lederer de Paris 165
Leiber, Judith 31, 32, 35, 39, 40, 45, 46, 166-173
Ley, Margaretha 123
Ley, Wolfgang 123
lizard skin 31, 32, 41, 170
Lucille de Paris 174, 175
metal 44-46
Missoni 62, 176
Missoni, Ottavio 176
Missoni, Rosita 176
Moskowitz, Morris 176, 177
ostrich feathers 43
ostrich skin 33, 34, 99, 132, 175
pigskin 152
Poiret, Paul 80
pony fur 9, 130
Prada 63, 177
Pucci di Barsento, Emilio 178, 179
Rodo 180
Rosenfeld, Harry 181
Rosenstein, Nettie 182-184
Sacha 34
silk fabric 36-40
snake skin 35, 52, 123, 169, 171, 172
Swarovski crystal 42, 45, 167
Tod's, J. P. Company 65, 185
tote bags 63-67, 189
travel bags 68-78
Valentino, 128, 129, see Garavani
Versace, Gianni 52, 77, 130, 185
Vuitton, Louis 55, 61, 186-188
Westwood, Vivienne 189

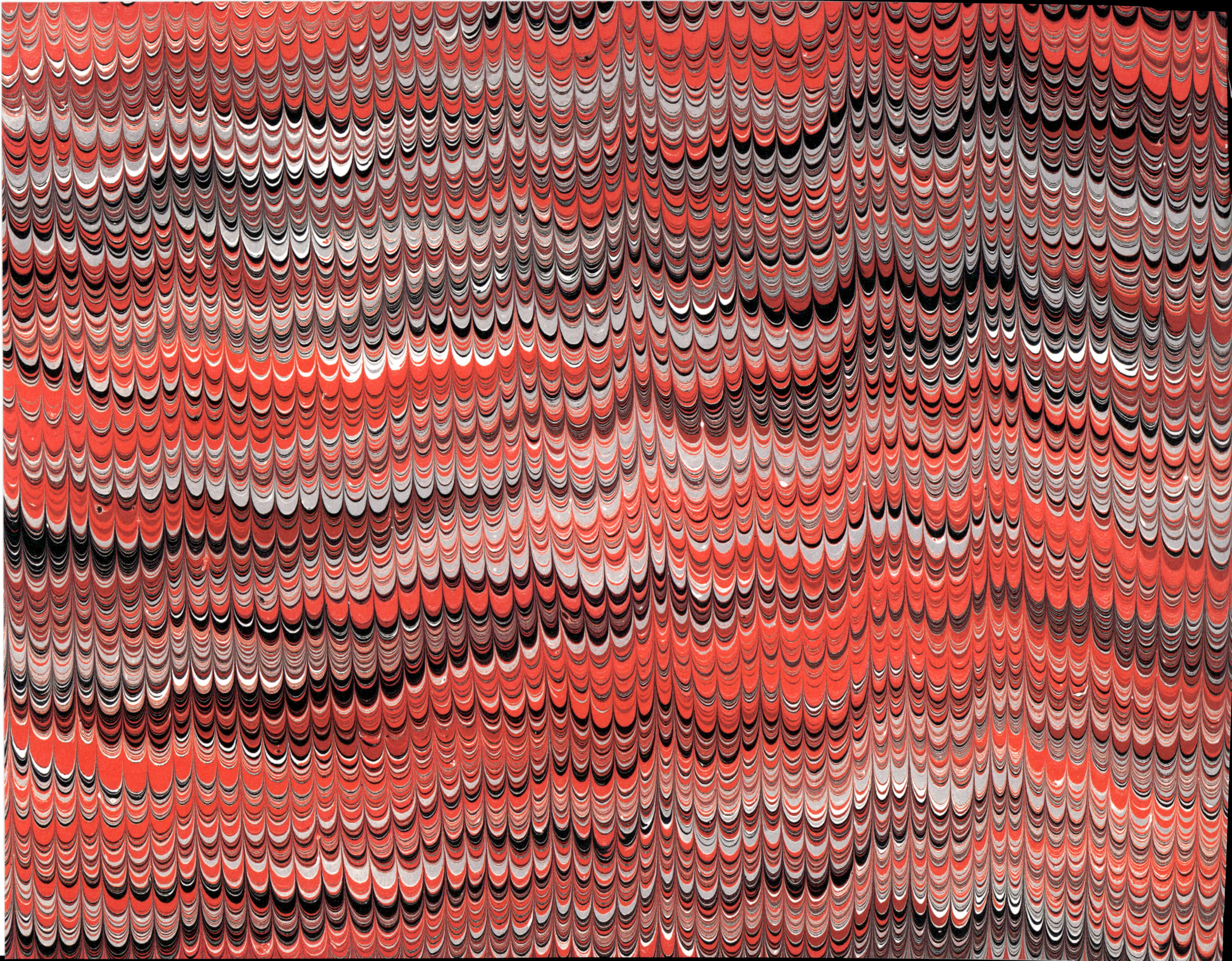